Everyone Disappears

poems by

W. Luther Jett

Finishing Line Press
Georgetown, Kentucky

Everyone Disappears

Copyright © 2020 by W. Luther Jett
ISBN 978-1-64662-372-3 First Edition
All rights reserved under International and Pan-American Copyright Conventions. No part of this book may be reproduced in any manner whatsoever without written permission from the publisher, except in the case of brief quotations embodied in critical articles and reviews.

ACKNOWLEDGMENTS

The author expresses his appreciation to the publishers of the following poems:

"Why the Ocean Tastes of Tears" appeared in *Wordwrights!* and in *Red Booth Review* (as "Todo el Mundo")
"Red Dirt", "Requiem", "Norway, Summer 2011" and "Days Like This" appeared in *JMWW*
"Seamus" appeared in *Potomac Review*
"Nightmares" appeared in the anthology, *Secrets and Dreams,* published by Kind of a Hurricane Press.
"Remembrance" appeared in the anthology *101 Jewish Poems for the Third Millennium*, published by The Ashland Poetry Press

In addition, "Hold / Let Go" received an Honorable Mention in the 2018 "Moving Words" contest poetry contest, sponsored by Arlington County, Virginia; "The Dreaming House" received a Laureate's Choice award in the 2018 Maria W. Faust Sonnet Contest. The author is grateful to the contest sponsors for their support.

Publisher: Leah Maines
Editor: Christen Kincaid
Cover Art: W. Luther Jett
Author Photo: Anonymous
Cover Design: Elizabeth Maines McCleavy

Order online: www.finishinglinepress.com
also available on amazon.com

Author inquiries and mail orders:
Finishing Line Press
P. O. Box 1626
Georgetown, Kentucky 40324
U. S. A.

Table of Contents

Nepenthe 1
Why the Ocean Tastes of Tears 2
The Sea House 3
Let The Dead Bury The Dead 4
Holding 5
Red Dirt 6
Monuments 7
Seamus 8
Days like This 9
Dear Sister 10
Nightmares 11
From A High Window 12
Summer Islands 13
Requiem 14
Norway, Summer 2011 15
That Night 16
Ashfall 17
Sanctum 18
Remembrance 19
Afternoon 20
Respite 21
Still 22
Coffin 23
Recollection Waltz 24
One By One 25
Home 26
Looking West 27
The Dreaming House 28
Before the Dawn 29
And The Gate Opens This Way 30
What We Could Not Keep 31
Hold / Let Go 32

Sing on, sing on you gray-brown bird,
Sing from the swamps, the recesses, pour your chant from the bushes,
Limitless out of the dusk, out of the cedars and pines.

—Walt Whitman, "When Lilacs Last in the Dooryard Bloom'd"

NEPENTHE

That time we were starving,
one of us died—I
don't remember
whether it was you or
me, but I'm certain
the disappearance tore a hole
in the continuum,
and it doesn't take much
now—fragment
of sky, a wall the colour
of sunflowers, that path
between the birches—miss
one meal and all the other
hungers rush in. Watch
night's fingers grip the naked
trees and see how lights
flicker on only to fade out again.
Yesterday I went
room to room, all through
the house, rifling drawers,
unsealing boxes, searching
for what cannot be found.
For what
I have forgotten.

WHY THE OCEAN TASTES OF TEARS
[For Perry Lindstrom]

Everyone goes away.
   Everyone disappears.
That should not surprise anyone.
It comes with the ticking of clocks
   in upstairs halls,
with the shadows of afternoons
   that turn golden before fading
and the last star left shining
   between the midnight west
     and bombdark dawn.
My mother cries at her kitchen sink
   and the girl I argued with
     washes out her paintbrushes
in a room I have never seen.
Voices fill the air.
   Small birds go south.
     The snow melts slowly.
Everyone disappears.
   When you most want them to stay
everyone goes somewhere
   else and that is why
     the ocean tastes of tears.
It's the one thing you can count on
   when you close your eyes—
     you dream and if
anyone is still there when you wake
   you've witnessed a revolution.

THE SEA HOUSE

Words pile up the way
old newspapers do
in a house of shuttered windows
on the edge of a chalk cliff
overlooking the sea,
newspapers no-one
reads any more, growing
brittle amid shadows.

Tiny granules of sand sift
through the cracks in the walls,
work their way
between the paper sheaves,
and if the house were an oyster,
there would be pearls.

And if I could
I would whisper these words
into the pearlpink shell of your ear,
send them sifting
down your long veins.
Let the shutters fall
from the windows of the house
waiting lonely by the sea.
Let the light in, let the wind
blow through.

LET THE DEAD BURY THE DEAD

Now, in the morning, lamps
light the long corridor.
New moon a pale circle,
sun a cipher.

Footsteps rustle among
dry weeds; breeze chills skin.
Forgotten toys, left
to sink into the lawn.

Old nursery rhymes,
scratched into a windowsill
with a rusted nail. A bookshelf
becomes an open door.

The clock has fallen
from the wall. Leaves
of the calendar fade.

Already, paper ghosts
are nailed by the gate.

Not all that's lost will be found.

HOLDING

Things shatter with the force of holding
too long in one place—ease up
on that throttle-grasp
before you choke. The air, that day,
was tuned a crystal-pitch,
and then, the smoke.
Paper-strips feathered from the sky, and on
each strip, a name enscribed.
If you paused to count them,
one by one, the dust
could swallow everything.

A word burns when held back,
as if a searing coal
lodged in the throat—cast down
from unimagined height.
And might one word atone
for everything?

Write this, then, in your ledger
where you keep your darker dreams—
After the lava cools
there is glass obsidian, smooth, black,
and keen, which gripped
too closely cuts
and red seeps over everything.

RED DIRT

This is the hell of it, the injury
becomes apparent in each step
across the beaten earth,
the wound we make of breathing.
There is no life which, in the end,
does not depend on death.

Carnivore cells
consume all in their paths; fungus
feeds upon decay; even flowers
cannot bloom by sunlight's
sole behest, requiring rot,
broken leaves and faded petals.

Do you imagine to do better
than the poppies of the field?
You who scatter seed
across continents? Each orgasm
is a little death. Each song
a requiem. Simply rising
of a morning is to undertake
a battle, pitched against unending night.
Red dirt collects
in every crevice of the skin
and never will scrub clean.

The soldier in his bivouac
dreams himself at war with time
and starts awake to scan
a ragged horizon, marking the slow
paling down the sky—neither
he nor I nor you can claim
to know the day ahead, although
the watcher on the border
watching back we know
well as we know our selves.

MONUMENTS

If a moment remains
frozen, it is no longer

A person looks up
seconds prior to erasure

Continents drift apart

Continents collide

When you whisper—Remember—
it is written on your grave

Do not rub it out
Do not rub it out

SEAMUS

At the banquet of the dead, I played
the stranger's banjo just as if
it was a friend, and you,
you were impossibly there and young,
whose face I last saw shaven grim
and boxed by time.

With one eye closed against the night,
I scanned the crowd to snatch
an image of the sun before
a gathering dust, before a wind
swept in to whisk the candles out
and bang the door.

Your broken flute strung on a nail,
that final glass cast to the floor,
its puddling dregs at last
gone dry with not a hand to shake
another drop from your
up-ended cup.

What can I sing to tell your feast?
I will not keen a dark-toned dirge;
instead, I'll harp by differing light
no wind can dim, no shroud
of dust conceal, nor ticking of
the clock toll out.

DAYS LIKE THIS

I.

On days like this—grey,
slick with rain,
smoke rises from chimneys,
fog congeals in the low places,
and it is not good to remember
other days like this.

II.

The trains that leave, never return.
Today my brother would have turned
fifty-six. He could not breathe
any longer. Days like this
steal the wind from among the branches.

III.

Hunger becomes a stone
which lies down and does not get up.
Smoke becomes a word
for that which cannot be spoken.
Fog covers it, a hand
pressing down on an open mouth.

IV.

I could wish another conclusion
but on days like this
everything silvers, monochrome, flat—
the smoke, the fog, the faces
of people on the streets are hidden.
There is no returning,
yet we are always looking back
over our shoulders. Inhale.
Exhale. Inhale.

DEAR SISTER

There is a photograph,
probably taken around 1954,
of me and Daddy
out on our front lawn.

Dad is cutting the grass
with a gas-powered push mower
—I remember it was deep green—
and I am running behind,
with a tiny toy lawn mower.

Our father—Then much younger
than either you or I are now.

I thought I had a copy,
but I can no longer find it—
still, it is locked in my memory.

Do you have a copy?
Oh, why would you?
Did it ever actually exist?

It is snowing here as evening
draws down its shade
and I am thinking of that
green day long gone.

The ground is so cold,
it is rapidly turning
white as Father's hair
the last time I saw him.

NIGHTMARES

My family has gone into town,
leaving me with the house
to myself. Dishes everywhere,
piles of laundry, books
scattered across the floor.

I am salvaging trinkets
from forgotten fairs.
The back door will not
stay closed. Something
out there wants in.

The wind picks up.
Snow covers the yard.
Trees lose their shapes,
the sky gone black.
I don't know where I am.

The dead return to life.
My mother saw them
walking on the ceiling
then went up
to speak with them.

When I was a child,
in the darkest night-hour,
the grandfather clock
at the foot of the stair
would move through our rooms

when it thought we were all asleep.

FROM A HIGH WINDOW

My mother is crying and stars
from a sky unexpectedly
broad murmur What
is all this about? She says
I'm going lots of places Don't
wait supper for me and from
a high window comes
the sound of coughing late
late in the carnival night
that no-one in the grey house can
explain and I a world
distant reach the bench
only after passing many doors
that open onto rooms I cannot
know and in them all
my mother lies weeping until
the stars go out

SUMMER ISLANDS

Between the great dunes
the wind stirs the tall grass—
A cry from a distant rookery
carried over cerulean waves.

The stones of the village
stand smothered by gorse—
The ever-changing sea
the colour of the sky.

A cemetery covered by sand
after a winter storm—
New graves dug out
above the ancient bones.

Evening mist erases the edge
between land and sky—
Empty black houses
will never tell their secrets.

REQUIEM

Somewhere in summer
we lost our virginity.

Was it under the yellow streetlamp,
where the moths beat their blind wings?

Or behind the door in the sound-wall
running longside the Interstate?

We blew past the last exit
for nowhere, heading beyond

the neon and all the fireworks.
The houses we were born in

will one day crumble to the touch,
vanishing as clouds

the way fireflies glimmer beneath
the dusky trees and are gone.

Moon-coloured graves yawn
atop the shrouded hills,

and the stars fall, the dawn
comes up, the long laziness

of mourning does not seem
the end of anything,

this dream no different
from the last, and yet entirely new.

NORWAY, SUMMER 2011

I do remember—it was
the summer before Mom died.

There had been a big explosion
and the city was covered in flowers—

Dead flowers, heaps of them
on every bridge and fountain.

Every staircase.
Every streetcorner.

And we were on a small boat,
going among the islands—

Summer cottages, white against
the green grass, scarred boulders.

Then we crossed the broad
bright bay to the farthest town

but there was no more time.
The cruise ship was set to sail.

To the north hung blue glaciers
amid silent crags, waiting

to be witnessed.

THAT NIGHT

the wind came through
she fell on the stairs
and all the lights went out
I started shaking
trees crashing down
I couldn't stop
darkness roared outside
until they brought me coffee
as the earth trembled
holding that cup of warmth
flickering flashlights
grounded me
in the silent room
monitor showed flat-line
nothing afterward the same
nothing afterward the same
leaves scattered across the lawn
all kinds of papers piling up
small branches, lines down
people stopping by
and this went on for days
the telephone kept ringing
all kinds of birds were flying
mornings were the worst
at some point realizing
I'd lost the shakes
the wind had stopped
the night remained

ASHFALL

In the night, ashes
fell until the park
was covered. We
kept breathing,
covering our mouths
with masks of damp
cotton. The heart's
roaring throb buried
speech. The room
grew smaller, the window
frosted over.

SANCTUM

A silence—dropt
amid the roar—
encompasses
a room apart——
If you would—enter
cautiously—
a sanctuary
without start
nor end nor any
in between
but an expanse—
more pale
than any snow's new-fallen
stillness
after winter's gale.

REMEMBRANCE

This is the suit
I only wear once a year,
if I'm lucky,
on Yom Kippur,
the Day of Remembrance.
My mother's house
sits entirely empty tonight.
Not even a cobweb remains,
and on Monday
the house will be sold
to a man I have not met
but who, I am sure, is kind.
The last time I spoke
with my mother was a long
and difficult phone call,
the threads of it
frayed and straggling.
I was about to ring off
when I remembered
to tell her I wouldn't be calling
the next Friday night.
"It will be Yom Kippur,"
I explained. "Yom Kippur,"
she repeated. Hours later,
my phone rang,
and it was not her,
and that was the year
I wasn't so lucky,
and wore this suit
more than once.

AFTERNOON

A stillness came without a word—
The restless trees no longer shook.
No traffic passed
and not a bird
cried out—The wind fell silent. Vast
and empty all the unbound land
seemed to me then—devoid of sound
or motion—for an Age.
Until with grace impenetrate
that stillness brushed my shoulder—
There—and softly urged me—
Wait.

RESPITE

I heard a bell toll in the noon
there by the stream beneath
the ruined wall,
and after—all the world was still,
the water cool in shadows green.

Now, as the summer's evening falls
down this dark grove across
the rock-bound sea,
and drumming of cicadas rings—
I wait beside the weathered door.

Many a moon between the now and then,
and many a sun to rise and fall;
roads upon roads that I have travelled down,
seas upon seas that I have yet to sail.

STILL

brushed cobalt clouds——ground
pale ochre——dimmed light——
children run bundled against
chill across the park——shrill
game of sevens——sun already
fallen late among bare trees——
tremor beneath sodden soil——
flutter of lamplight

my brother would still not yet be sixty

COFFIN

When you are fearful
of being forgotten
you become a box
that can only hold
so much—Understand,
the walls are not solid.
Water seeps in.
The wind blows between
the holes in our skin.
Our eyes met once.
Nothing after
has been the same.

RECOLLECTION WALTZ

I remember the feel of flowers,
dusky to the touch, their fresh
scent in April, after the rain.

And how the bees of summer hovered
by the blooming rose, a wing-stirred
breeze brushing my cheek.

The green-dappled forest.

Morning breaking over fields.

Those were the ways we counted
our breaths, between the rising
and the fall, a long, slow dance.

Then the lanterns, strung beside
the path between the trees,
floated up to meet the stars.

There, we could not follow.

Nor speak again the same heart.

ONE BY ONE

First to go
was the town library,
eaten by fire—each burnt
book a world lost. Then,
the apartments I cohabited
with cockroaches, bulldozed
to make way for a new city.

All the places I
once breathed and walked,
vanishing, one by one.

Next, the old high school—
classrooms, book closets,
locker-rooms, brick by brick,
laid to rubble. My parents' home
gutted, made over,
and now I cannot bear
to drive past.

Paper disintegrates, stone
wears away. What remains?
I chant the names of things
long after they have gone,
one by one—book, bed,
desk, brick, tree, street,
mother, father.

HOME

When I said, "I want to go home,"
I meant the opposite.
I was crying on the road, yes,
between one place and
another, the sky was blue, even so,
what I meant was the opposite.

When I said, "I want to go home,"
I meant, "I do not need
"to return," because I have crossed
oceans to dwell among
strangers, and now the faces of home
are gone alien and give
no comfort. What I meant was,
"You can't go back there."

I was crying, yes, but when I said,
"I want to go home,"
I meant, "Bring out the dead." I meant
to say, "The house
has fallen in that once was home."
The sky is still blue,
and when I said, "I want to go home,"
I meant, "I have no mother."

LOOKING WEST

I will never sit again
where the window looks out
toward the river,
never while winter trees shake bare
beneath the western wind, nor while
April's small rains lace the land.

Here in a room my age, I crane
my neck to watch the sun
drop behind black trunks and know
that where it sinks the same
broad river runs.

And all that was has gone
for dust, and all that will
shall also fade,
while the sober sun metes out our days,
our autumn fogs, our summer's
haze, the crisp circumference of years.

Over green hills the wild deer run,
the crows may make their dinner
sweet; the sky from red to umber rolls,
as lamps come up to light the way
down to the hidden shore.

THE DREAMING HOUSE

The children who grew in that house now dark,
who rambled over field and sunbright hill,
are gone to shadowed streets. They left their mark
beside the stone-bound path. The air is still.

With morning there will come the song of birds
to break the silent reverie of night;
unspoken thoughts give birth to living words
as larks and sparrows in their joy take flight.

And then the long-locked door at last shall creak
upon its hinge. The wind will stir the dust
that lingers on the sill. The walls will speak
as dawn revives the quick and wakes the just.

This is the dream that murmured, ages gone—
Our end is not in twilight, but in dawn.

BEFORE THE DAWN

From the dark beside this
empty road: a voice
the colour of crystal, of ice
hung from the winter eave.

After a time untolled, over a
distance unfathomed: a thin
sliver of blue slips upward
out of the unmarked earth.

When we are gone, a radiant
miasma will encompass this territory.

The featureless black plain
will dissolve into undifferentiated
       expanse.

From this new day here until
that new day there, runs a thread:
       Forgiveness.

AND THE GATE OPENS THIS WAY

The sun chooses not to answer
my letter scrawled in the sand.

The stone calendar collapses.
I can no longer focus my eyes.

Everything recedes from everything else.
Even the sea has left the shore behind.

The little foxes have entered the arbor.
In the north, bomb shelters are sealed.

Soon there will be nothing to sing for,
only the carolina wren who darts

in and out among the green boughs
in spite of everything.

Her wings stir the air the way
my fingers once stirred sand.

The mute sun expands
beyond the bending cedars.

The sky is not a wall but a gate
left swinging open by an unseen hand.

WHAT WE COULD NOT KEEP

Summer porches wrapped
round shingle-fronted
rooms—aroma
of strawberries warm
from the garden out back.

Roadside dust raised
on dry days to settle
silver among ragged
robins—air thick
with thunder's promise.

Rusted cattleguards,
bleachboard racks
for milk-cans—unseen
trains slow as they pass
through brickyard towns.

Cicada's cry.

A thousand wings
cross the sky at dusk.

Toy lost in new-mown
field—old dog
settled in shade—
fear-tinged chill,
sudden bee's hum.

HOLD / LET GO

There is darkness and there
is light. Somewhere
dawn opens the sky even
while here night closes her fist.

No eye is shut so tight
a star's kiss won't pierce it.

W. Luther Jett is a native of Montgomery County, Maryland. His poetry has been published in numerous journals, including *The GW Review, Beltway Poetry Quarterly, Innisfree, Potomac Review, Little Patuxent Review, Rockburst Review, District Lit, Footnote, Third Wednesday, Words + Pictures, JMWW, Tuck Magazine, Algebra of Owls, Lines & Stars,* and *Main Street Rag*. His poems have also appeared in several anthologies, including *My Cruel Invention* (Meerkat Press, 2015), Element(ary)*My Dear* and *Secrets and Dreams* (both from Kind of a Hurricane Press, 2015 & 2016) and *Proud to Be* (Southeast Missouri State University Press, 2013).

He is the author of two poetry chapbooks: *Not Quite: Poems Written in Search of My Father*, [Finishing Line Press, 2015], and *Our Situation*, [Prolific Press, 2018].

Jett's poem "Holding" received an honorable mention in 2015 from Delaware Literary Connections. His poem "Love Song for a Dismembered Country" was selected as a finalist in the *Third Wednesday* Poetry Contest in 2018. Recently, Luther received an Honorable Mention in the 2018 Moving Words Poetry Contest for his poem, "Hold / Let Go". He was also a winner in the 2011 Moving Words Poetry competition in Arlington, VA. His sonnet, "The Dreaming House" was awarded a "Laureate's Choice" in the 2018 Maria W. Faust Sonnet Contest.

Jett's poetry performance piece, *Flying to America*, debuted at the 2009 Capital Fringe Festival in Washington D.C. He is also the facilitator of a bi-annual open mike sponsored by the Hyattstown Mill Arts Project in Hyattstown, Maryland, as well as a monthly poetry workshop which meets the first Saturday of every month at the Kensington Book Store, Kensington, Md.

www.ingramcontent.com/pod-product-compliance
Lightning Source LLC
LaVergne TN
LVHW041600070426
835507LV00011B/1219